Let's Keep in Touch

Follow Us

Visit US at

www.learnpersianonline.com

Call

1-469-230-3605

Online

 www.facebook.com/PersiaClubCo

 www.twitter.com/PersiaClub

 www.instagram.com/LearnPersianOnline

Online Persian Lessons Via Skype

It's easy! Here's how it works.

1- Request a FREE introductory session.

2- Meet a Persian tutor online via Skype.

3- Start speaking Real Persian in Minutes.

Send Email to: info@LearnPersianOnline.com

Or Call: +1-469-230-3605

www.learnpersianonline.com

... So Much More Online!

- **FREE Farsi lessons**

- **More Farsi learning books!**

- **Online Farsi – English Dictionary**

- **Online Farsi Tutors**

Looking for an Online Farsi Tutor?

Call us at: 001-469-230-3605

Send email to: Info@learnpersianonline.com

Farsi Crossword Puzzles

Truly pleasant puzzles for Farsi learning

1

By

Reza Nazari

www.LearnPersianOnline.com

Copyright © 2018 Reza Nazari

Printed in the United States of America

All rights reserved.

No part of this publication may be reproduced, stored in a retrieval system, or transmitted in any form or by any means, electronic, mechanical, photocopying, recording, scanning, or otherwise, except as permitted under Section 107 or 108 of the 1976 United States Copyright Ac, without permission of the author.

All inquiries should be addressed to:

info@learnpersianonline.com

www.learnpersianonline.com

ISBN-13: 978-1725728905

ISBN-10: 1725728907

Published by: Learn Persian Online Website

www.LearnPersianOnline.com

About the Author

Reza Nazari is a Persian author. He has published more than 100 Persian learning books including:

- Learn To Speak Persian Fast series,
- Farsi Grammar in Use series,
- Persia Club Dictionary Farsi – English,
- Essential Farsi Idioms,
- Farsi Verbs Dictionary
- Read and Write Persian Language in 7 Days
- Laugh and Learn Farsi: Mulla Nasreddin Tales For Intermediate to Advanced Persian Learners
- Farsi Reading: Improve your reading skill and discover the art, culture and history of Iran
- and many more ...

Reza is also a professional Farsi teacher. Over the past eight years, his online Persian lessons have helped thousands of Persian learners and students around the world improve their language skills effectively.

To participate in online Persian classes or ask questions about learning Persian, you can contact Reza via email at: reza@learnpersianonline.com or his Skype ID: rezanazari1

Find Reza's professional profile at:
www.learnpersianonline.com/farsi-tutor-reza

Contents

- Description 9
- Pronunciation Guide 10
- Persian Alphabet 12
- Colors 16
- Animals 19
- Clothes 23
- Weather 27
- Around the Home 30
- Body 34
- Family 38
- Foods 41
- Numbers 44
- Sports 48

Description

Designed for Farsi learners who want to improve their language skills, crossword puzzles in this book give you a deserved break from drill books. Offering different ways to learn more than 200 Farsi words, these themed crossword puzzles will challenge and entertain you! These are truly pleasant, if not addictive, puzzles for Farsi learning.

Farsi Crossword Puzzles offers an entertaining way for Farsi learners to sharpen their word skills while they solve pleasant crossword puzzles. It provides fun and easy-to-follow puzzles for all ages and ability levels.

If you are a Farsi learner needing more practice, *Farsi Crossword Puzzles* is the perfect answer to making learning Farsi an engaging experience! You can hone your language skills with this entertaining workbook.

Studying Farsi language does not have to be boring!

Pronunciation Guide

The regular letters used for written Persian stand for some different sounds. It is usually difficult to tell how a word is pronounced just by looking at how it is spelled. Therefore, it is useful to show the pronunciation of each word separately, using a system of symbols in which each symbol stands for one sound only. After each verb in this book, the word is given again within two slashes to show its pronunciation.

This book uses a simple spelling system to show how verbs are pronounced, using the symbols listed below.

Symbol	Example	Symbol	Example
a	hat /hat	m	move /muv
â	cut / cât	n	need /nid
ay	time /tâym	o	gorgeous /gorjes
ch	church /cherch	ô	coat/ côt
d	dog /dâg	u	mood /mud
e	men /men	p	park /pârk
ey	name /neym	r	rise /rais
f	free /fri	s	seven /seven
gh	similar to "r" in French	sh	shut /shât
h	his /hiz	t	train /treyn
i	feet /fit	v	vary /vari
iyu	cute /kiyut	y	yet /yet
j	jeans /jinz	z	zipper /ziper
k	kettle /ketl	zh	measure /mezher/
kh	loch /lakh	'	تعظیم /ta'zim
l	loss /lâs		

Persian Alphabet

The Persian alphabet (الفبای فارسی) consists 32 letters, most of which have two forms, short and full. It is a writing style based on the Arabic script. The Persian script is entirely written cursively. That is, the majority of letters in a word connect to each other. Some of the letters are similar in shape but differ in the place and number of dots. Some others have the same sound but different shape.

Following is a table showing the Persian alphabet and how it is pronounced in English. There are also some examples of how those letters would sound if you place them in a word.

	Farsi Alphabet			آلفبای فارسی	
Row	Letters	Pronunciation	Sample	Pronunciation	Meaning
1.	آ - ا	alef	آب	āb	water
2.	بـ - ب	be	بابا	bābā	father
3.	پـ - پ	pe	پاپ	pāp	the pope
4.	تـ - ت	te	تاب	tāb	swing
5.	ثـ - ث	se	اَثاث	asās	furniture
6.	جـ - ج	jim	تاج	tāj	crown
7.	چـ - چ	che	چای	chāi	tea
8.	حـ - ح	he	حَج	haj	pilgrimage
9.	خـ - خ	khe	خانه	khāneh	home
10.	د	dāl	دَرد	dard	pain
11.	ذ	zāl	جَذب	jazb	absorption
12.	ر	re	دَر	dar	door
13.	ز	ze	میز	miz	table
14.	ژ	zhe	ژاپُن	zhāpon	japan
15.	سـ - س	sin	اُستاد	ostād	professor
16.	شـ - ش	shin	دانشجو	dāneshjoo	student
17.	صـ - ص	sād	صَد	sad	hundred
18.	ضـ - ض	zād	وُضو	vozu	ablution

	Farsi Alphabet				آلفبای فارسی

Row	Letters	Pronunciation	Sample	Pronunciation	Meaning
19.	ط	tā	طَناب	tanāb	rope
20.	ظ	zā	ظُهر	zohr	noon
21.	عـ - ع	eyn	عَدَد	adad	number
22.	غـ - غ	gheyn	شُغل	shoghl	job
23.	ف - ف	fe	دَفتَر	daftar	notebook
24.	ق - ق	ghāf	قَهوه	ghahveh	coffee
25.	ک - ک	kāf	کِتاب	ketāb	book
26.	گ - گ	gāf	دانشگاه	dāneshgāh	university
27.	ل - ل	lâm	کِلاس	kelās	classroom
28.	مـ - م	mim	مات	māt	blur
29.	نـ - ن	nun	نان	nān	bread
30.	و	vāv	وان	vān	bath
31.	هـ ـهـ ه	he	ماه	māh	moon
32.	یـ - ی	ye	نیم	nim	half

Colors		رنگ ها /ranghâ/
English	Pronunciation	Persian
White	sefid	سفید
Blue	âbi	آبی
Green	sabz	سبز
Brown	ghahve'i	قهوه ای
Gray	khâkestari	خاکستری
Orange	nârenji	نارنجی
Violet	banafsh	بنفش
Red	ghermez	قرمز
Yellow	zard	زرد
Black	siyâh	سیاه

Colors / رنگها

۱	۵	۹	
۲	۶	۱۰	
۳	۷ سفید		
۴	۸		

ر	ن	ک	ج	ق	ب	ژ	ن	پ	آ
ش	ا	پ	ش	ف	ن	ب	م	ن	د
ث	ر	د	ی	ف	س	م	ی	م	ر
ی	ن	ق	د	ش	ی	و	ز	ق	ن
ط	ج	غ	ت	ب	ن	ر	غ	ج
ه	ی	ا	ه	و	ق	د	ا	ی
ق	چ	ح	ص	م	ن	د	م	ی	ط
ر	ی	چ	خ	ا	ک	س	ت	چ	ه
م	ن	د	ی	ب	آ	ق	ز	ی	ق
ز	و	ر	ژ	ز	ط	ه	ظ	غ	ر

Colors / رنگها

بنفش	قهوه ای	✓ سفید
قرمز	خاکستری	آبی
	نارنجی	سبز
	زرد	سیاه

Animals

حیوانات
/heyvânât/

English	Pronunciation	Persian
Deer	âhu	آهو
Horse	asb	اسب
Tiger	babr	ببر
Goat	boz	بز
Bird	parande	پرنده
Crocodile	temsâh	تمساح
Donkey	khar	خر
Bear	khers	خرس
Rabbit	khargush	خرگوش
Giraffe	zarâfe	زرافه
Dog	sag	سگ
Lion	shir	شیر

Animals		حیوانات /heyvânât/
English	Pronunciation	Persian
Eagle	oghâb	عقاب
Elephant	fil	فیل
Cow	gâv	گاو
Cat	gorbe	گربه
Wolf	gorg	گرگ
Snake	mâr	مار
Mouse	mush	موش
Monkey	meymun	میمون

Animals — حیوانات

۱	....	۵	....	۹	....
۲	....	۶	....	۱۰	....
۳	خرگوش	۷	....	۱۱	....
۴	....	۸	....		

```
ر  ن  ک  ج  خ  و  ه  آ
ش  ه  د  ن  ر  پ  ب  م
ی  ر  د  ت  ب  ا  ق  ع
ر  ن  ق  م  ر  ی  ر  ت
ط  ج  ب  س  ا  ت  ن  ج
ل  ی  ف  ا  ز  ب  ق  د
و  ا  گ  ح  ز  ب  ن  ق
ط  چ  ن  ق  س  ر  خ  خ
```

حیوانات	Animals		
آهو	پرنده ✓	شیر
اسب	تمساح	عقاب
ببر	خر	فیل
بز	خرس	گاو

Clothes

لباس ها
/lebâshâ/

English	Pronunciation	Persian
Shirt	pirâhan	پیراهن
Tie	kerâvât	کراوات
Dress	lebâs	لباس
Blouse	boluz	بلوز
Suit	koto shalvâr	کت و شلوار
Skirt	shalvâr	دامن
Coat	kot	کت
Jacket	zhâkat	ژاکت
t-shirt	tishert	تی شرت
Pants	shalvâr	شلوار
Short	short	شرت
Pullover	poliver	پلیور

English	Pronunciation	Persian
	Clothes	**لباس ها** /lebâshâ/
Glove	dastkesh	دستکش
Pajama	pijâme	پیجامه
Socks	jurâb	جوراب
Shoe	kafsh	کفش
Boot	chakme	چکمه
Slipper	dampâyi	دمپایی
Hat	kolâh	کلاه
scarf	shâl	شال

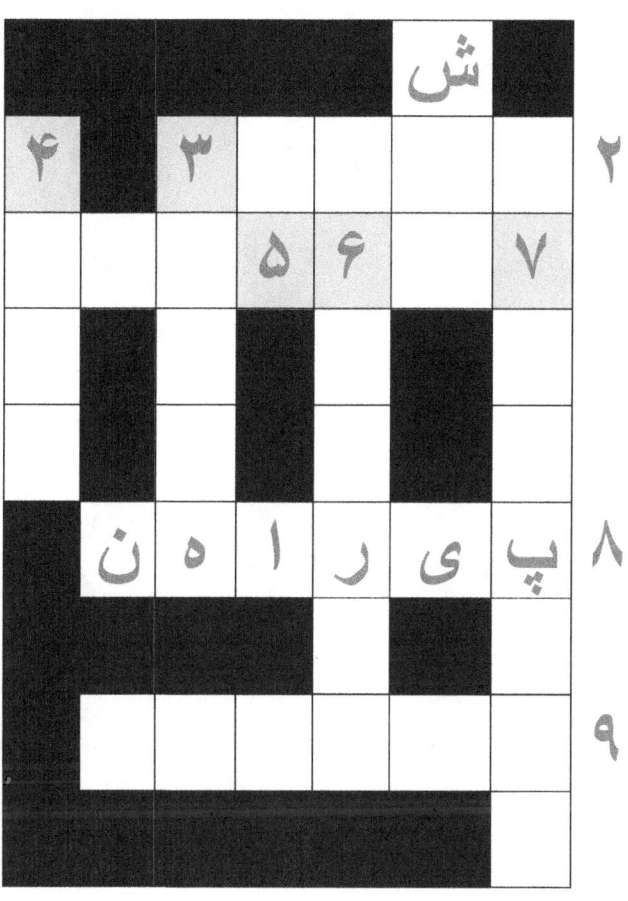

لباس ها — Clothes

۱ .... ۴ .... ۷ ....

۲ .... ۵ .... ۸ پیراهن

۳ .... ۶ .... ۹ ....

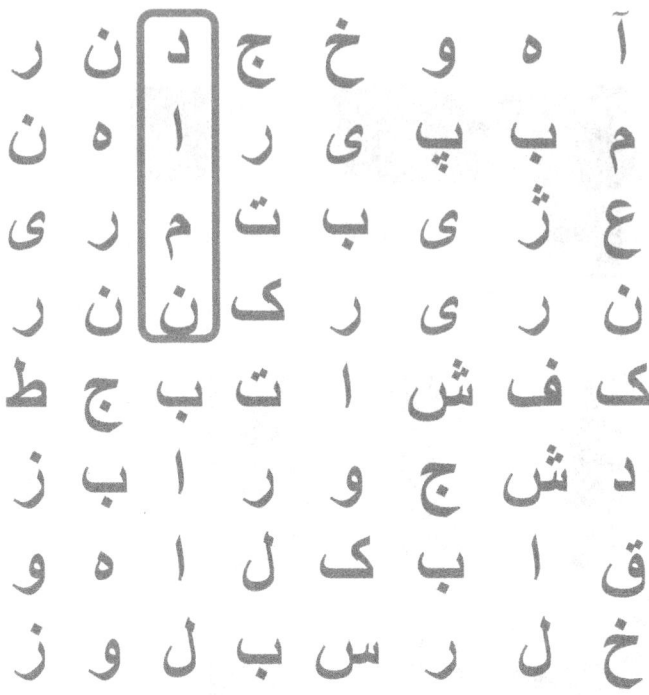

Clothes   لباس ها

جوراب   پیراهن
کفش   ✓ دامن
کلاه   بلوز
شال   کت

English	Pronunciation	Weather	آب و هوا /âbo havâ/ Persian
rain	bârân		باران
snow	barf		برف
cloud	abr		ابر
sun	âftâb		آفتاب
fog	meh		مه
wind	bâd		باد
storm	tufân		طوفان
thunder	ra'do bargh		رعد و برق
cold	sard		سرد
warm	garm		گرم
rainbow	rangin kamân		رنگین کمان

Weather   آب و هوا

۱ طوفان   ۴ ....   ۷ ....

۲ ....   ۵ ....

۳ ....   ۶ ....

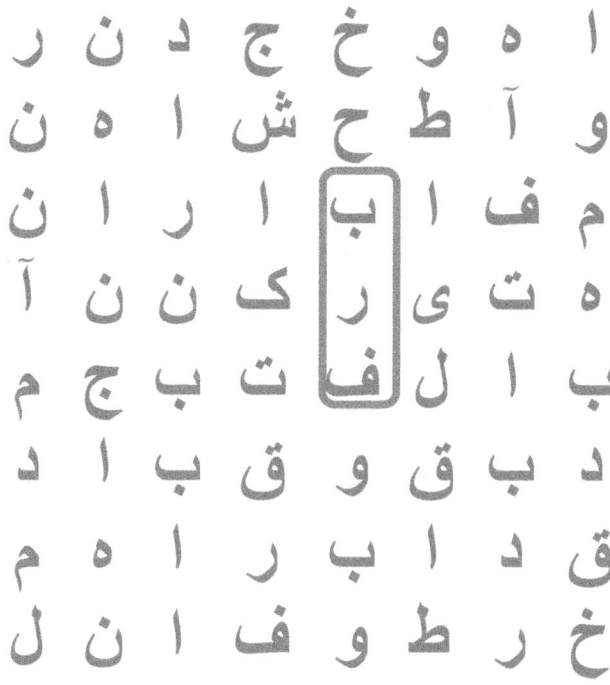

Weather   آب و هوا

آفتاب   باران

طوفان   ✓ برف

مه   ابر

       باد

Around the Home		در خانه /dar khâne/
English	**Pronunciation**	**Persian**
Sofa	mobl	مبل
Refrigerator	yakhchâl	یخچال
Table	miz	میز
Window	panjere	پنجره
Computer	kâmpiyuter	کامپیوتر
Oven	ojâgh	اجاق
Chair	sandal	صندلی
Door	dar	در
Bed	takhtekhâb	تختخواب
Rug	ghâli	قالی

Around the Home

در خانه
/dar khâne/

English	Pronunciation	Persian
Shelf	ghafase	قفسه
Television	telveziyon	تلویزیون
Cabinet	kâbinet	کابینت
Mirror	âyine	آیینه

Around the home — در خانه

١ .... ۴ .... ۷ ....

٢ .... ۵ پنجره

۳ .... ۶ ....

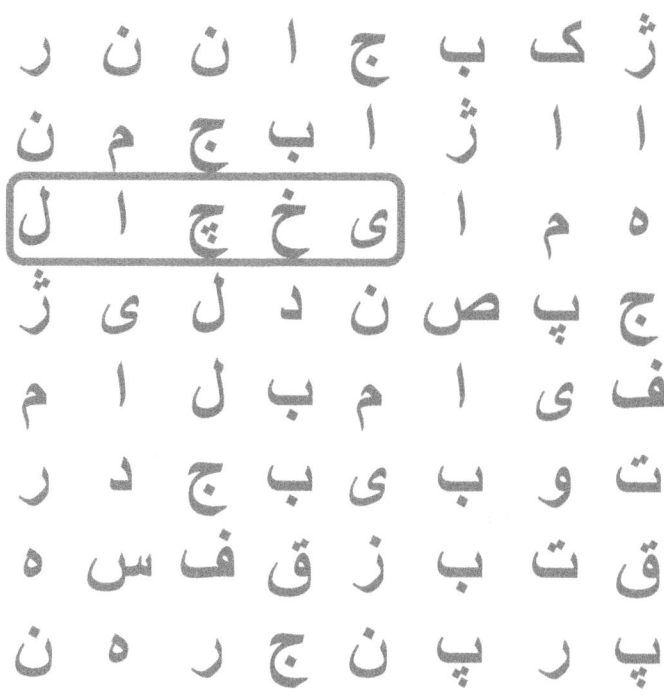

در خانه　　　　　　　Around the Home

✓ یخچال　　　　　میز
مبل　　　　　　پنجره
صندلی　　　　　کامپیوتر
در　　　　　　　قفسه

	Body	بدن /badan/
English	**Pronunciation**	**Persian**
Head	sar	سر
Eyebrow	abru	ابرو
Eye	cheshm	چشم
Mouth	dahân	دهان
Finger/Foe	angosht	انگشت
Chin	châne	چانه
Hair	mu	مو
Leg	pâ	پا
Forehead	pishâni	پیشانی
Nose	damâgh	دماغ
Hand	dast	دست
Neck	garden	گردن

Body
بدن
/badan/

English	Pronunciation	Persian
Ear	gush	گوش
Eyelash	mozhe	مژه
Shoulder	shâne	شانه
Stomach	shekam	شکم

Body   بدن

١ .... ۴ .... ۷ .... ۱۰ ....

٢ .... ۵ .... 8 ....

٣ .... ۶ .... 9 چشم

ش	و	گ	خ	و	پ	ب	د
م	ه	ا	ر	ی	ب	د	ق
ن	ا	ه	د	ت	ش	ر	خ
ژ	ی	ک	ی	غ	ا	م	د
و	ر	ب	ا	م	ن	ی	ف
ز	م	ش	چ	و	ی	ش	د
و	ه	ل	ا	پ	ب	ا	ق
ز	و	ب	م	ر	ل	خ	

بدن Body

پیشانی   دهان
دماغ   ابرو
پا   چشم
مو   ✓ گوش

Family

خانواده
/khânevâde/

English	Pronunciation	Persian
Mother	mâdar	مادر
Father	pedar	پدر
Brother	barâdar	برادر
Sister	khâhar	خواهر
Grandfather	pedar bozorg	پدربزرگ
Grandmother	mâdar bozorg	مادربزرگ
Son	pesar	پسر
daughter	dokhtar	دختر
children	bachehâ	بچه ها

Family   خانواده

۱ .... ۴ .... ۷ ....

۲ .... ۵ .... 8 ....

۳ .... ۶ مادربزرگ

```
د  ک  ب  ج  د  خ  ت  ر
ق  ا  ژ  پ  ب  ر  ر  ه
خ  م  ا  د  ج  ه  ا  ک
م  ا  د  ر  ب  ز  ر  گ
ا  ی  ب  ر  ا  د  ر  ر
د  و  ب  ی  ا  ش  ش  ه
ر  ت  ق  پ  س  ر  ا  ک
خ  و  ا  ه  ر  ب  ی  ر
```

	Family		خانواده
	پسر		مادربزرگ
	خواهر		مادر
			پدر
		✔	برادر

Foods

خوردنی ها
/khordanihâ/

English	Pronunciation	Persian
Sandwich	sândevich	ساندویچ
Spaghetti	mâkârâni	ماکارانی
Eggs	tokhme morgh	تخم مرغ
Chicken	morgh	مرغ
Milk	shir	شیر
Cheese	panir	پنیر
Ice cream	bastani	بستنی
Rice	berenj	برنج
Bread	nân	نان
Salad	sâlâd	سالاد
Butter	kare	کره
Chocolate	shokolât	شکلات
Coffee	ghahve	قهوه
Tea	chây	چای
Cake	keyk	کیک
Cookies	shirini	شیرینی

Foods   خوردنی ها

١ .... ۴ .... ۷ ....

٢ .... ۵ .... 8 ....

۳ ماکارانی   ۶ ....   ۹ ....

پ	ب	خ	ج	خ	د	ر
ا	ر	ی	پ	ر	ا	ه
م	ش	چ	و	ی	ن	د
ق	ج	ب	س	ت	ن	ی	ن
ب	پ	ا	و	چ	ی	و	ک
ی	ش	ک	ل	ا	ت	ژ	ط
ب	پ	ر	س	ا	ل	ا	د
ر	م	ه	چ	ا	ی	ر

خوردنی ها   Foods

کره   سالاد
شکلات   چای
✓ بستنی
برنج

www.LearnPersianOnline.com   43

Numbers		اعداد /a'dâd/
English	**Pronunciation**	**Persian**
ziro	sefr	صفر
One	yek	یک
Two	do	دو
Three	se	سه
Four	chehâr	چهار
Five	panj	پنج
Six	shesh	شش
Seven	haft	هفت
Eight	hasht	هشت
Nine	noh	نه
Ten	dah	ده
Eleven	yâzdah	یازده
Twelve	davâzdah	دوازده

Numbers

اعداد
/a'dâd/

English	Pronunciation	Persian
Thirteen	sizdah	سیزده
Fourteen	chehârdah	چهارده
Fifteen	pânzdah	پانزده
Sixteen	shânzdah	شانزده
Seventeen	hefdah	هفده
Eighteen	hejdah	هجده
Nineteen	nuzdah	نوزده
Twenty	bist	بیست

اعداد		numbers	
۱	5	9	13 ....
۲	6	10	
۳	7	11	
۴ سیزده	8	12	

ا د ج د ن ر ا ر ب
و ش پ ه ش ت ص پ
م ا ا ن ا ب ی س ت
ه ز ب ج د ه ب ی و
ب د و ا ز د ه ز م
د ه ب ا ر ا ب د ه
پ ا ن ز د ه پ ه ژ
د ق و خ م ا د ر ن

	Numbers	اعداد
	دوازده	پنج
	سیزده	هشت
✓	پانزده	نه
	بیست	ده

English	Pronunciation	Persian
	Sports	ورزش ها /varzeshhâ/
Badminton	badminton	بدمینتون
baseball	beysbâl	بیسبال
Volleyball	vâlibâl	والیبال
Billiard	biliyârd	بیلیارد
boxing	boks	بوکس
Swimming	shenâ	شنا
Chess	shatranj	شطرنج
Cricket	keriket	کریکت
Cycling	docharkhe savâri	دوچرخه سواری
Dart	dârt	دارت
Golf	golf	گلف
Gymnastics	zhimnâstik	ژیمناستیک

Sports

ورزش ها
/varzeshhâ/

English	Pronunciation	Persian
Hacky	hâki	هاکی
Jogging	do	دو
Soccer	footbâl	فوتبال
Basketball	basketâl	بسکتبال
Wrestling	koshti	کشتی
Karate	kârâte	کاراته
Football	footbâle âmrikâyi	فوتبال آمریکایی

ورزشها   Sports

۱ ژیمناستیک   ۴ ....   ۷ ....

۲ ....   ۵ ....   8 ....

۳ ....   ۶ ....

ژ	ط	ه	ر	ک	ن	ه	و
ا	ب	ا	ر	ا	ن	ن	ف	ص
ی	ر	ک	ش	ت	ی	ک	و	ت
آ	ف	ت	ی	ر	ک	ن	ت	ت
ا	د	ب	ج	ن	ر	ط	ش	ت	ه
ا	ا	ر	ا	ی	ت	ه	ن	ف	ص
ف	ل	گ	ا	ت	ر	ا	د	ت
ر	ر	ب	پ	ژ	ا	ق	و	ی

ورزش ها — Sports

شطرنج	فوتبال
شنا	کشتی ✓
دارت	هاکی
دو	گلف

Answers

Colors

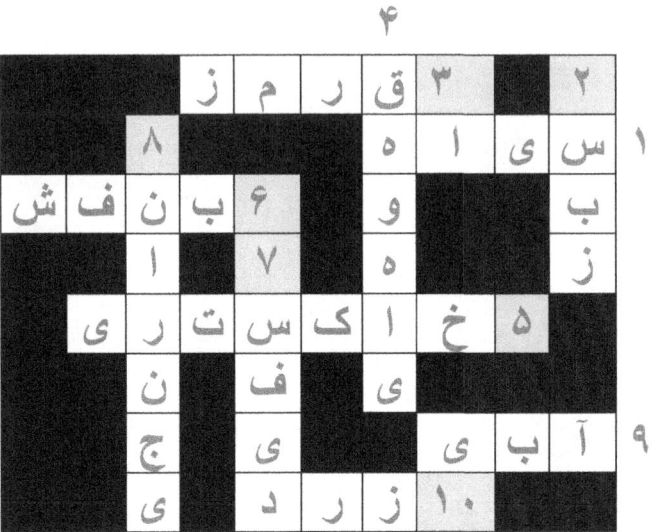

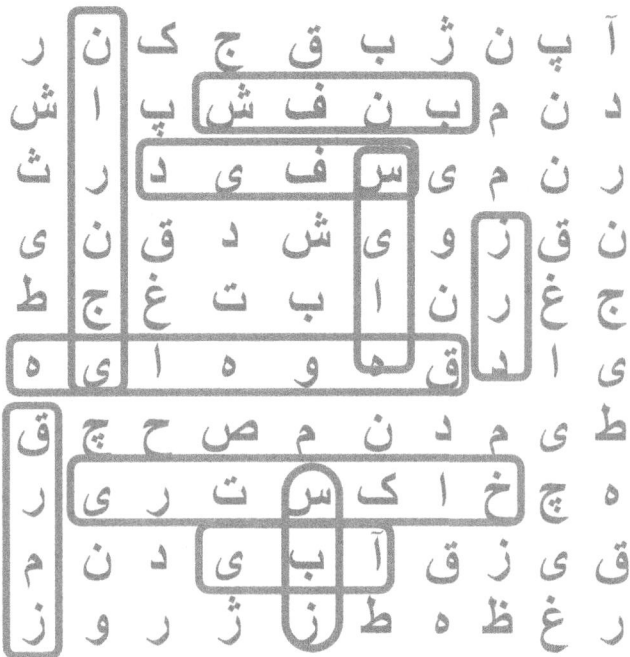

Animals

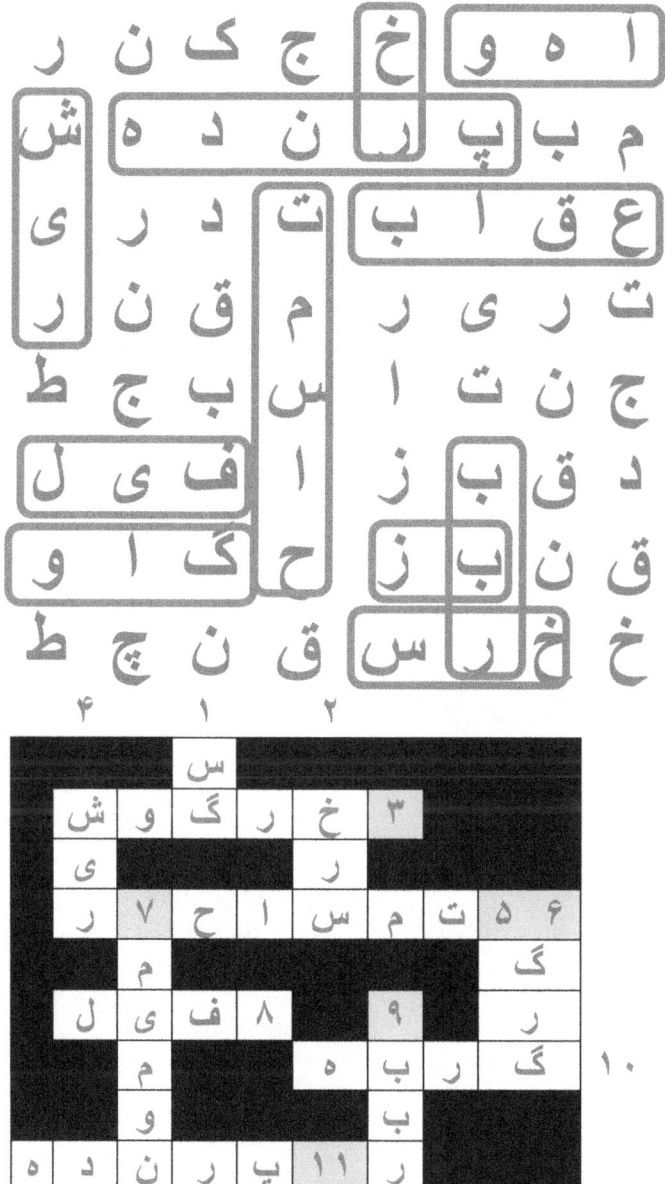

Clothes

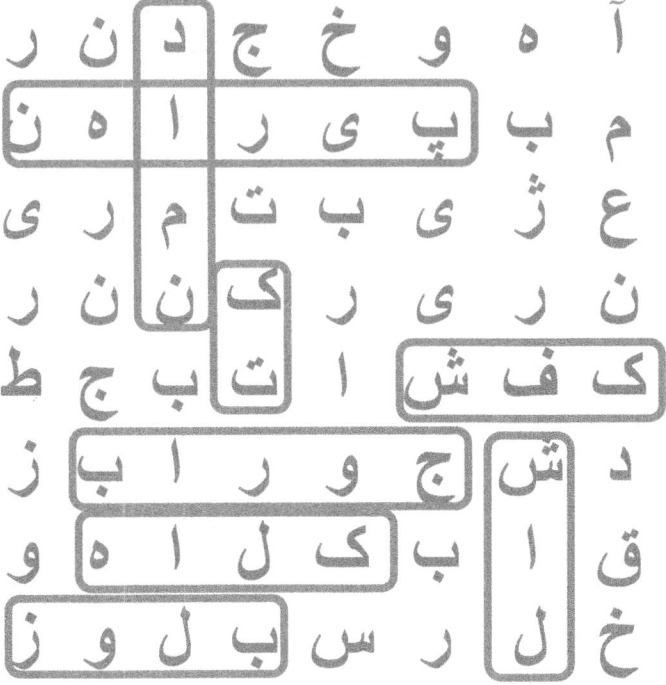

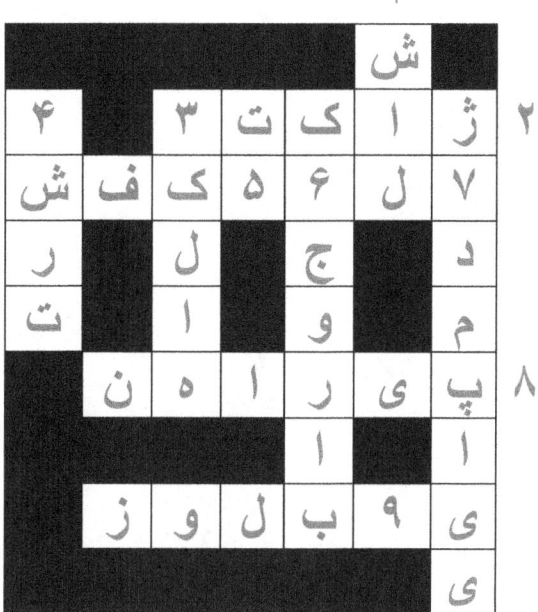

Weather

Around the Home

Body

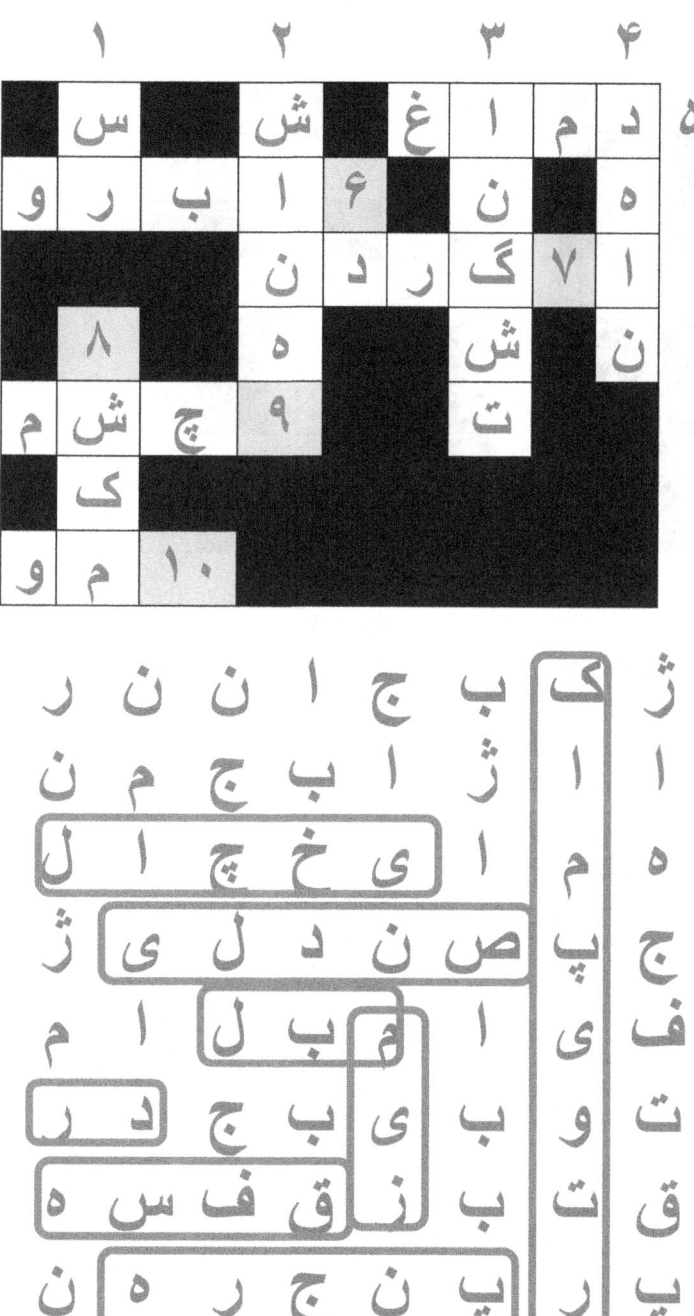

www.LearnPersianOnline.com

Family

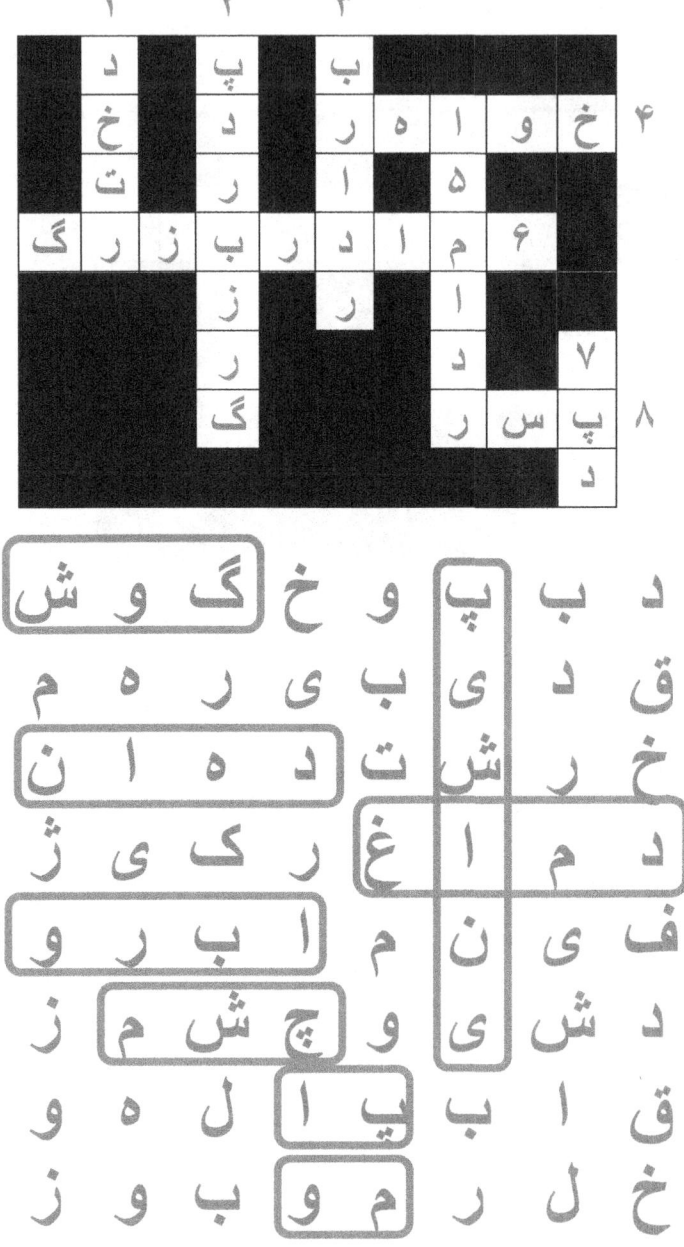

Foods

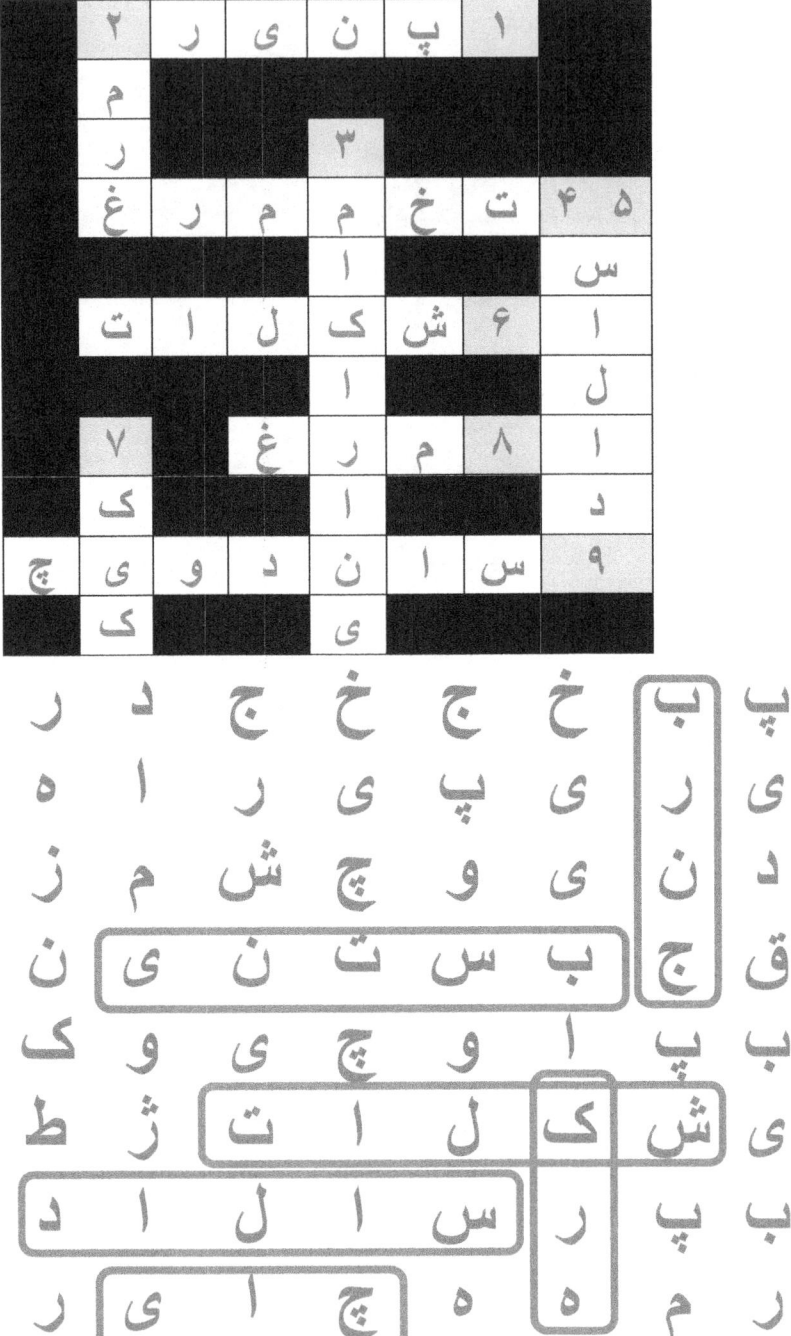

Numbers

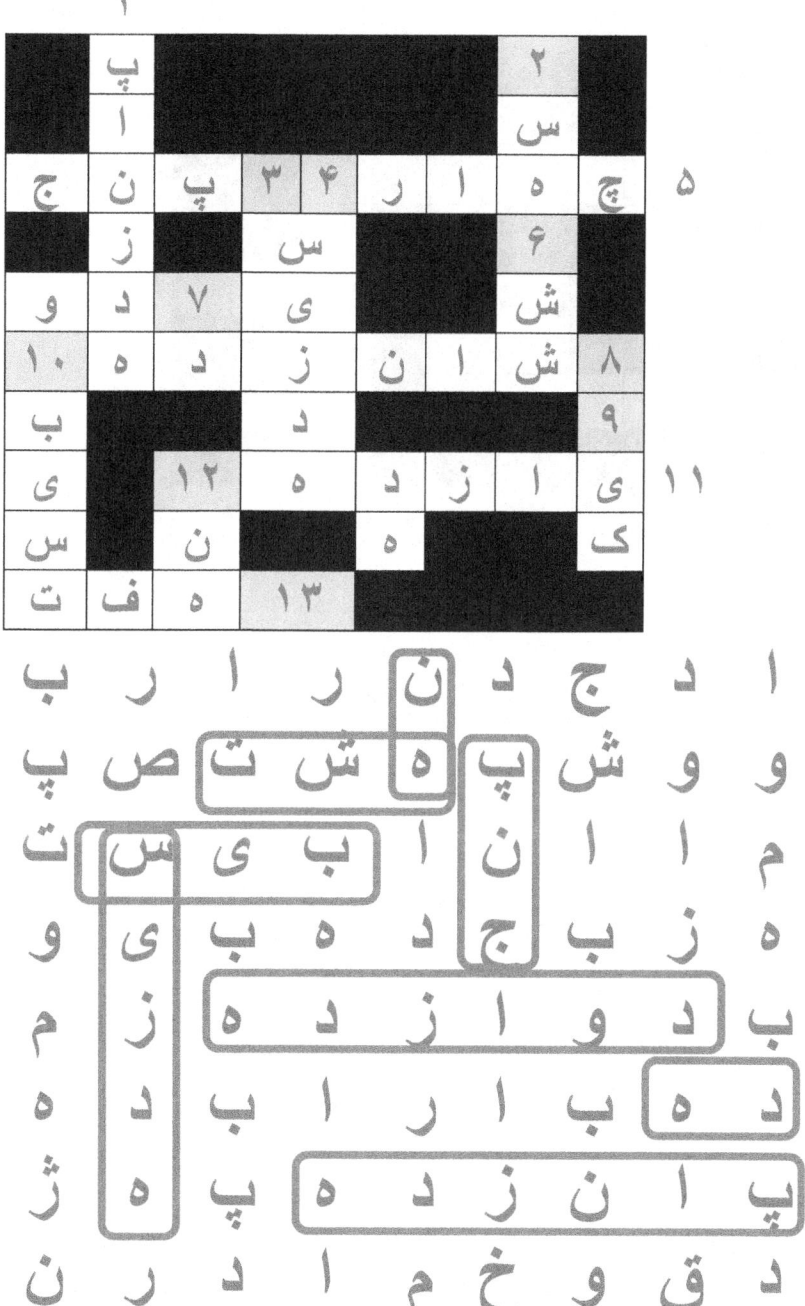

Sports

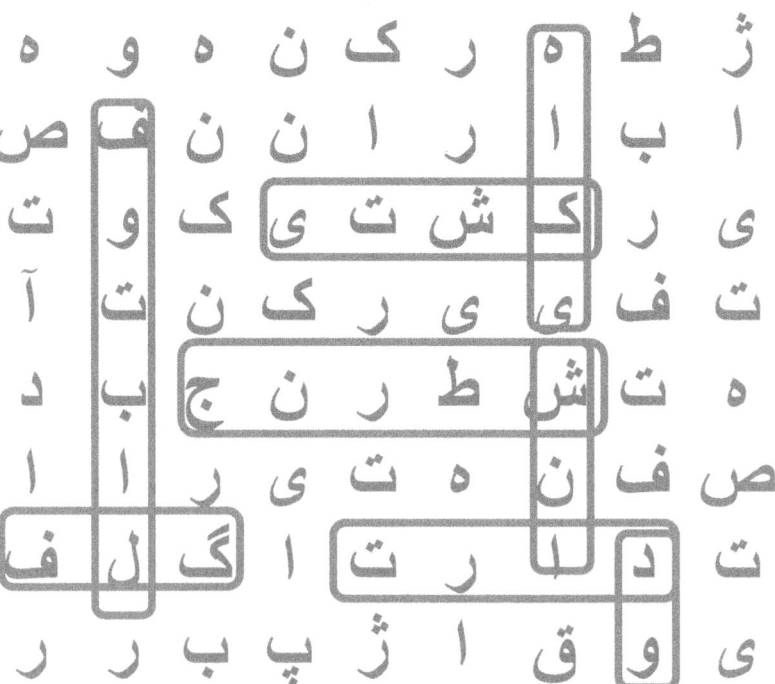

Other Books of Interest

Learn Farsi in 100 Days
The Ultimate Crash Course to Learning Farsi Fast

The goal of this book is simple. It will help you incorporate the best method and the right strategies to learn Farsi FAST and EFFECTIVELY.

Learn Farsi in 100 days helps you learn speak Farsi faster than you ever thought possible. You only need to spend about 90-120 minutes daily in your 100-day period in order to learn Farsi language at advanced level. Whether you are just starting to get in touch the Farsi language, or even if you have already learned the basics of the language, this book can help you accelerate the learning process and put you on the right track.

Learn Farsi in 100 days is for Farsi learners from the beginning to the advanced level. It is a breakthrough in Farsi language learning — offering a winning formula and the most powerful methods for learning to speak Farsi fluently and confidently. Each contains 4 pages covering a comprehensive range of topics. Each day includes vocabulary, grammar, reading and writing lessons. It gives learners easy access to the Farsi vocabulary and grammar as it is actually used in a comprehensive range of everyday life situations and it teaches students to use Farsi for situations related to work, social life, and leisure. Topics such as greetings, family, weather, sports, food, customs, etc. are presented in interesting unique ways using real-life information.

Purchase on Amazon website:

https://goo.gl/eG2n11

Published By:
Learn**Persian**Online.com

Easy Persian Phrasebook

Persian for Busy Travelers

101 Most Common Persian Words

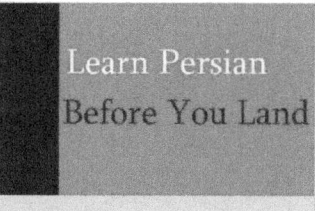

Learn Persian before You Land

Top 1500 Persian Words

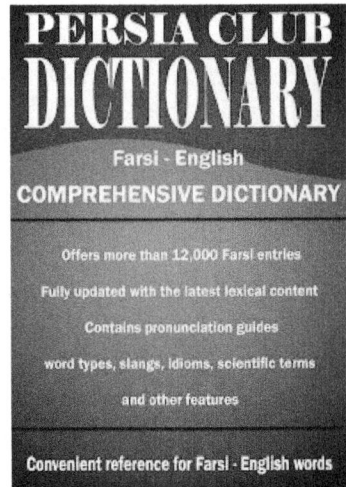

Persia Club Dictionary Farsi - English

Persian For Travel

Effortless Persian Alphabet

Laugh and Learn Farsi

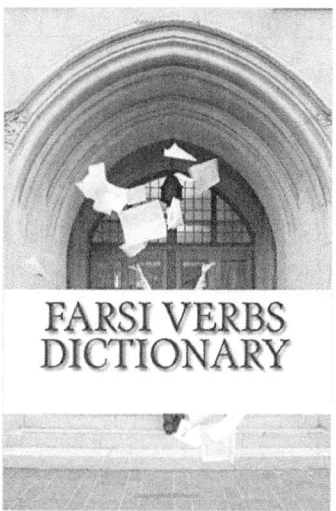
Farsi Verbs Dictionary

Essential Idioms In Farsi

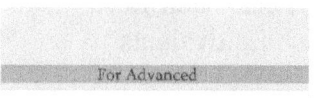

Farsi Reading

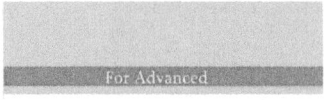

101 Most Common Farsi Proverbs and Their Best English Equivalents

Farsi Reading

Farsi Grammar in Use: For beginners

Easy Persian Crossword Puzzles

"Learn Persian Online" **Publications**

"Learn Persian Online" authors' team strives to prepare and publish the best quality Persian Language learning resources to make learning Persian easier for all. We hope that our publications help you learn this lovely language in an effective way.

Please let us know how your studies turn out. We would like to know what part of this book worked for you and how we can make this book better for others. You can reach us via email at info@learnpersianonline.com

We all in *"Learn Persian Online"* wish you good luck and successful studies!

"Learn Persian Online" Authors

www.learnpersianonline.com

⋯ So Much More Online!

- ✓ FREE Farsi lessons
- ✓ More Farsi learning books!
- ✓ Online Farsi – English Dictionary
- ✓ Online Farsi Tutors

Looking for an Online Farsi Tutor?

Send email to: Info@learnpersianonline.com

Made in United States
Orlando, FL
13 June 2025